MY FIRST LOOK AT VEHICLES

**SOME BOATS ARE MADE OF SMOOTH WOOD**

# Boats

## CATHY TATGE

CREATIVE EDUCATION

Published by Creative Education

P.O. Box 227, Mankato, Minnesota 56002

Creative Education is an imprint of The Creative Company

Designed by Rita Marshall

Photographs by Steven J. Brown, Bruce Carr, Corbis (Archivo Iconografico, Bettman, Edward

S. Curtis, Hulton-Deutsch Archive, C.E. Kelly, David Lees), Cunard, Herbert L. Gatewood,

Getty Images (The Image Bank), Anne Gordon, Hulton Archive, Derk R. Kuyper, Sally McCrae

Kuyper, North Wind Picture Archives (N.C. Wyeth), D. Jeanene Tiner, John Wilson

Printed in the United States of America

**Library of Congress Cataloging-in-Publication Data**

Tatge, Cathy. Boats / by Cathy Tatge.

p. cm. — (My first look at vehicles)

Includes index.

ISBN-13: 978-1-58341-526-9

1. Boats and boating—Juvenile literature. 2. Ships—Juvenile literature. I. Title. II. Series.

VM150.T37 2007      623.82—dc22      2006027447

First edition 9 8 7 6 5 4 3 2 1

# BOATS

## Splash!

Boats are vehicles that float on water. They rock back and forth on windy days. Boats move with the water. You can hear the waves sometimes. They splash against the boat.

Boats can carry people or things. Some boats have **engines** to help them move. Engines can make a boat go fast.

MANY BOATS HAVE A NAME PAINTED ON THEM

Other boats use sails to move. Sails are big pieces of cloth that catch the wind. The wind pushes the boat through the water.

Sometimes people move boats with oars. Oars are long sticks that have one flat end. The flat end pushes the water and moves the boat.

The *Titanic* was a famous
cruise ship. It hit an **iceberg**
in the ocean and sank.

THE *TITANIC* SANK ALMOST 100 YEARS AGO

## Boats Long Ago

People used boats more than 6,000 years ago. In Egypt, people used boats on the **Nile River**. They fished from them.

The first boats were small. But soon people began to make bigger boats. The bigger boats could sail on the ocean.

Native Americans used
canoes. Canoes are boats
that are long and narrow.

BOATS WERE SOME OF THE FIRST VEHICLES

Christopher Columbus was an **explorer**. He wanted to find a way to China. He sailed on the ocean for two months. He did not find a way to China. Instead, he found North America. He went back to Europe and told everyone about this new land. Soon, many people took boats to North America.

## Boats That Work

Today, boats do many jobs. Some people use boats for fishing. They use small boats on lakes and ponds. Big boats are used on

Christopher Columbus had
three boats. They were named the
*Niña*, the *Pinta*, and the *Santa Maria*.

the ocean. These boats carry many things across the ocean. They can move clothes, food, and even cars!

Cruise ships are huge boats that people take trips in. Many cruise ships have places to eat and swimming pools. A cruise ship is like a city that floats.

CRUISE SHIPS CAN CARRY THOUSANDS OF PEOPLE

Barges are big boats. They can carry many things. Barges are so big that they need another boat to help them move. Tugboats are small boats, but they are strong. One small tugboat can pull a big barge!

## Boat Ride

It is fun to ride in boats. But it is important to follow the rules of safety. People should always wear life jackets when they ride in small boats. Life jackets help people float if they fall in the water.

The front of a boat is
called the bow. The back
of a boat is the stern.

**TUGBOATS HELP BIGGER BOATS STEER AND MOVE**

Some big boats have windows in the bottom of the boat. People can see the fish and plants in the water below! Other boats are small. There is room for only two or three people to sit down.

People have used boats for a long, long time. When you follow the rules of safety, it is fun to ride in boats!

LIFE JACKETS HELP PEOPLE IN BOATS TO STAY SAFE

# Hands-on: Build a Boat

Make your own boat and see how it floats!

## What You Need

Modeling clay
A bathtub or bowl
Water

## What You Do

1. Fill the tub or bowl with water.
2. Roll the clay into a ball.
3. Put the ball in the water. Does it float?
4. Flatten the clay and turn up the sides. Make the clay look like a boat.
5. Put the boat on the water. Does it float?

The shape of a boat helps it float. The boat-shaped clay has more space for the water to push against. This makes the boat float.

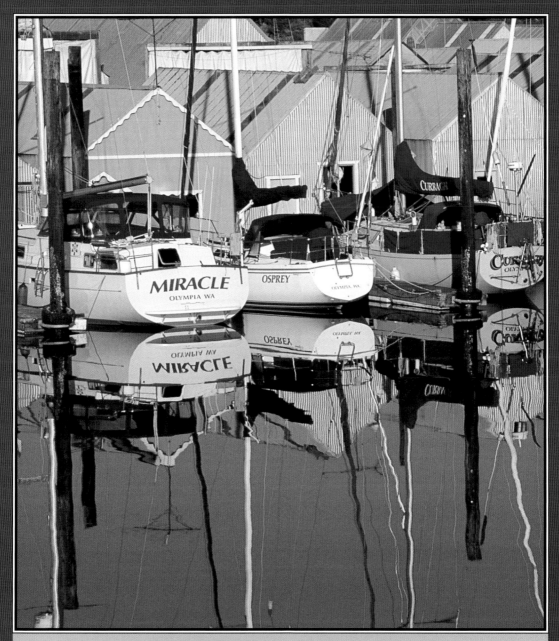

**BOATS COME IN MANY SHAPES AND SIZES**

## Index

## Words to Know

**engines**—machines that make boats move

**explorer**—a person who searches for new places

**iceberg**—a big piece of ice in the ocean

**Nile River**—the longest river in the world; it is in Africa

## Read More

Barton, Byron. *Boats*. New York: HarperCollins, 1998.

Holtzman, Robert. *Boats & Ships: Your Field Guide*. North Kingstown, R.I.: Moon Mountain, 2004.

Mitton, Tony. *Busy Boats*. Boston: Kingfisher, 2005.

## Explore the Web

**Boat Safe Kids** http://boatsafe.com/kids/index.htm

**Coastie's Homepage** http://coastie.auxpa.org/

**Safe Boating Kidsite** http://www.boatingsidekicks.com/kidsite/ contest-index1024.htm